Advent Calendar Colouring Book

24 numbered Christmas colouring pages,
one for each day of Advent.

***

Lindsay Small

Small Publishing Ltd, Office SO177, 265-269 Kingston Road, Wimbledon, London SW19 3NW

www.smallpublishing.co.uk

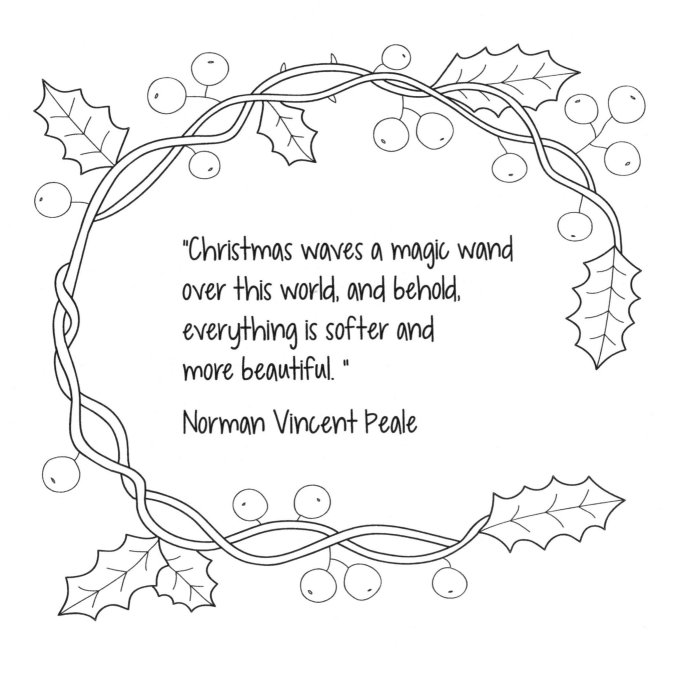

"Christmas waves a magic wand over this world, and behold, everything is softer and more beautiful. "

Norman Vincent Peale

Advent Calendar Colouring Book

Turn the pages to find 24 lovely Christmas colouring pages, one for each day of Advent.

I've spaced the colouring pages so that you can cut them out for display if you choose.

If you are using felt-tip pens you may want to place a piece of card behind the page you are working on, to minimise the chance of bleed through. Flip to the back of the book to find a test page to try out your colours.

Happy colouring, and best wishes for the holiday season!

Merry Christmas!

Test Your Colours Here

For more colouring pages for children (and adults) as well as thousands of puzzles, worksheets and other fun printable activities for kids, please visit my website, www.ActivityVillage.co.uk.

Made in the USA
Coppell, TX
24 October 2021

64605904R00037